A COMPANION GUIDE TO

The Jesus Creed

A COMPANION GUIDE TO

The Jesus Creed

Scot McKnight

PARACLETE PRESS
BREWSTER, MASSACHUSETTS

September 2004 Second Printing
August 2004   First Printing

© 2004 by Scot McKnight
ISBN 1-55725-412-5
10 9 8 7 6 5 4 3 2

Published by Paraclete Press
Brewster, Massachusetts
www.paracletepress.com

Printed in the United States of America.

In *The Jesus Creed: Loving God, Loving Others* I ask one simple question: what did Jesus mean by spiritual formation? The Christian world is abuzz with suggestions: some of them classical and some of them brand new. But, we need to ask, how would Jesus have defined spiritual formation. The answer is clear: Jesus expressed his view of spiritual formation in the ancient categories of his own heritage. That heritage expressed the fundamental relationship to God in what is now called the *Shema*: "Hear, O Israel: the LORD our God, the LORD is one. Love the LORD your God with all your heart with all your soul and with all your strength" (Deuteronomy 6:4-5). This is what Jesus learned from his father and mother, and it is what he passed on to his own followers. With one breath-taking amendment: "The second is this: 'Love your neighbor as yourself.' There is no command-ment greater than these" (see Mark 12:31). What remains when all is shaken down is this: love God and love others.

So, according to Jesus, the fundamental characteristic of a person who is spiritually formed is this: such a person loves God (by following Jesus) and loves others. To love God by following Jesus, and to love others, means also that a spiritually formed person embraces the stories of others who live out the *Jesus Creed*. I gave as illustrations of such stories, the examples of Joseph, Mary, Peter, John, and the women of compassion. Those who love God and love others have a third characteristic: they live out the kingdom values of that *Jesus Creed*. Kingdom values are hard to purchase in the modern moral market place: they include total transformation; the mustard seed principle (the little deed is the large act);

and the restoration of persons to society, joy, and an eternal perspective on their present life.

Because of who Jesus is, two more characteristics are notable: a spiritually formed person loves Jesus personally and participates in his very life. Loving Jesus involves trusting him, abiding in him, surrendering to him, being restored to him when we fail, forgiving others, and reaching out with the good news of the kingdom. Again, because of who Jesus is, his life could be uniquely lived for others. In *The Jesus Creed: Loving God, Loving Others* I went through six events in the life of Jesus, illustrating how each of those events was an act of love by Jesus for us: his baptism, his temptation, his transfiguration, his last supper, his death, and his resurrection.

Whenever a sweep of Jesus' life and teachings is made, many items are left untouched. So, I am asking you to pick up some of those pieces yourself either through personal study or joining with others like you who want to learn more about the *Jesus Creed*. This *Companion Guide* is designed to enable readers of *The Jesus Creed* to deepen their love of God and love of others in a variety of ways. It is written for groups but can easily be adapted by individuals who prefer to study each session alone.

The ideal posture

To benefit from the *Companion Guide* it is best if each person has a Bible, *The Jesus Creed* book, the *Companion Guide*, and a pen and paper. Spend a few minutes "centering down" (as the Quakers say) to find that inner quiet that prepares us both to speak with *Abba* and to hear from *Abba*. Since the *Companion Guide* is designed for a group to reflect together on the reading, and on other biblical passages, it is important to be receptive to whatever the Spirit might say.

The question of time

How long might it take to do a lesson? This question is often asked of those who lead retreats and who write about spiritual formation. The answer is predictable: time is not the issue. The *Companion Guide* is constructed to help people hear from God and to help them consider changes. Sometimes we will hear from God quickly; at other times we will not. Sometimes our world will be shaken; other times it will not be. Sometimes we will brush against Eternity in a solemn, barely detectable moment. At other times, we may struggle for days, weeks, or even months. This is how spiritual formation occurs. There are no magical formulas for communion with *Abba*. Take all the time you need. Often you may find that the group session will not be enough; you will want to spend some time alone, in the privacy of your home, pondering items that have entered into your heart.

The wise know that what we read and what enters our mind and heart, over time, forms us spiritually. So, be less concerned with the time it takes or obtaining immediate results than with enduring shifts in the mind and heart. Our concern is to fill ourselves with the wholesome splendor of God's Word, for it is in contact with God that our lives are spiritually formed.

Having said that, I believe that each session in the *Companion Guide* can be completed in a group session together, though some may find themselves so enrapt in prayer or meditation on a scriptural text that time will seem both to stand still and pass in a flash. Because of time constraints some may find they will only complete part of each exercise. This is fine; we are in no hurry. We are trying to hear from God. For that we have plenty of time.

Basic format

The *Companion Guide* has a basic format: each session begins with reciting the *Jesus Creed* and ends with reciting the Lord's Prayer. In between, each session works through the following: formation principle, formation prayer, formation exercises, and (for those who want to extend the session) further exploration.

The *formation principle* is a summary of the theme of a single chapter in *The Jesus Creed*. Someone in the group may want to summarize the chapter in more detail, while someone else might want to do the same for the Gospel passages shaping each chapter. Some groups may wish to begin by reading the Gospel readings under the chapter title of each chapter in *The Jesus Creed*.

The *formation prayer* can be prayed aloud, or silently, and can be adjusted to meet the needs of the group. The *formation prayer* is designed to turn each chapter of *The Jesus Creed* into a brief prayer.

The *formation exercises* are a step-by-step process of internalizing the *formation reflection* and the *formation prayer*. Genuine progress can be made by the genuinely honest. Truthtelling is a non-negotiable factor for all spiritual growth because we are dealing here with our deepest selves. For genuine spiritual formation to occur, each of us needs to be ready to change.

In each *spiritual exercise* I recommend that groups "identify together" specific personal connections to the *formation reflection*, "reflect together" on specific items suggested from the chapter, "listen" individually to what the Lord might be saying, and "imagine" as specifically as possible how to integrate what is being learned. "Imagining" is important because the *Jesus Creed* teaches that we are to love God with our minds. To do this, we must let our minds ruminate, meditate, contemplate, and cogitate (to use the classic words). We are to let our minds wander into the wilds of God's grace. To do this, we must "imagine." We can be surprised how much of faith begins with imagination—with vision and with wonder. Spiritual directors ask students to grow by changing, so the *Companion Guide* as a final group exercise will ask each of us to "commit" to new behaviors as an experiment of faith.

The *further exploration* section is designed for a group (if there is time), but it will be especially helpful for the individual who wants to follow up the group session with deeper study. The *further exploration* section focuses primarily on the Gospels since the concern of *The Jesus Creed* and this *Companion Guide* is how Jesus understood spiritual formation. I have no expectations that each person will ponder each passage each day. The various passages are given as suggested readings. Many find that "journaling" both intensifies and solidifies the session. To "journal" one needs simply to write out, usually in a notebook, dedicated exclusively to spiritual journaling, what comes to mind during the session.[1]

Reading a chapter is rarely enough for any of us. This *Companion Guide* has one central aim: to help each of us deepen the *Jesus Creed* into the soul of our being, to rub it into the tissues of our heart, and so to let it shape our entire life. In both *The Jesus Creed* and the *Companion Guide* I urge each of us to learn to recite the *Jesus Creed* as a daily rhythm. I know from experience that it can become what Evelyn Underhill called a "prayer of aspiration," that is, the frequent and attentive use of little phrases of love and worship, which help us, as it were, to keep our minds pointing the right way, so that these little phrases never lose their power of forming and maintaining in us an adoring temper of soul. . . . The habit of aspiration is difficult to form, but once acquired exerts a growing influence over the soul's life.

Precisely. The *Jesus Creed* can be just that: a rhythmical prayer of aspiration. All day long.

---

[1] Some examples include Evelyn Underhill, *Fragments of an Inner Life: The Notebooks of Evelyn Underhill* (ed. D. Hill; Harrisburg, Penn.: Morehouse, 1993); C. S. Lewis, *All My Road Before Me: The Diary of C. S. Lewis, 1922–1927* (New York: Harcourt Brace Jovanovich, 1991); Alexander Schmemann, *The Journals of Father Alexander Schmemann, 1973–1983* (Crestwood, N.Y.: St. Vladimir's Seminary Press, 2000).

T H E   *J E S U S   C R E E D*
"Hear, O Israel,
the Lord our God, the Lord is one.
Love the Lord your God with all your heart,
with all your soul,
with all your mind, and with all your strength."
The second is this:
"Love your neighbor as yourself."
There is no commandment greater than these.

CHAPTER 1

The *Jesus Creed*

"The best use of life is love.
The best expression of love is time.
The best time to love is now."
—Rick Warren, *The Purpose-Driven Life*, p. 128.

Recite the *Jesus Creed* together

FORMATION PRINCIPLE:
*Spiritual formation is about loving God
and loving others. In particular, loving God means to
follow Jesus personally.*

FORMATION PRAYER:
Abba, *quicken my heart so that I may love you
and others by following Jesus.
Drive from my heart any unworthy loves.
Through Jesus Christ. Amen.*

FORMATION EXERCISES:

- IDENTIFY TOGETHER how some of your favorite Christian writers conceptualize the Christian life or spiritual formation. (Give concrete examples.) How does one's conceptualization actually shape that formation?

- REFLECT TOGETHER on how the *Shema* of Judaism (Deuteronomy 6:4–9) and the *Jesus Creed* are similar and how they differ. What is the significance of the differences? What is the value of memorizing and reciting the *Jesus Creed*? What do you learn about the *Jesus Creed* from the statement above by Rick Warren?

- LISTEN to what God is saying to you about loving him and loving others. *Hear* the word of Jesus: "Come, follow me" (Mark 1:17a). How is this a form of loving God?

- IMAGINE your life—with your family, with your co-workers, and with your church community—as a life dedicated to loving God and loving others. What could that life look like today and tomorrow?

- COMMIT your lives to the *Jesus Creed*—to loving God and to loving others.

Recite the Lord's Prayer together

FURTHER EXPLORATION

Ponder the following persons who were challenged by the call of God to live out the *Jesus Creed*. Individuals may want to *journal* some reflections.
- Joseph (Matthew 1:18–25) • Mary (Luke 1) • Peter (Luke 5:1–11)
  • Matthew (Matthew 9:9–13) • Women (Luke 8:1–3)

C H A P T E R   2

Praying The *Jesus Creed*

"Through prayer God involves us
in the process of decision making
whereby things happen in the world."
—John Goldingay, *Walk On*, p. 46.

Recite the *Jesus Creed* together

F O R M A T I O N   P R I N C I P L E :
*The Lord's Prayer is a prayer that shapes
our love for God and others.*

F O R M A T I O N   P R A Y E R :
Abba, *give us love, love for you and for others.
Show us your love, show us the love of your Son for us,
and show us how we might love others. Turn our love for
you and others into prayer, the kind of prayer
that honors your Son. Through Jesus, the Lord. Amen.*

FORMATION EXERCISES:

- IDENTIFY TOGETHER how the Lord's Prayer is connected to the *Kaddish*. How does the Lord's Prayer express the *Jesus Creed*? *Identify together* how your prayers are grouped—are they grouped around God's glory and petitions for others?

- REFLECT TOGETHER on some public prayers in your church community. How do they reflect the Lord's Prayer as love for God and for others? *Reflect together* on John Goldingay's statement above: How is prayer an action? How does it prompt action? How is the story about Mike Breaux a good example of the Lord's Prayer?

- LISTEN to what the Spirit is prompting you to ponder about your prayer life.

- IMAGINE the prayers of the Church as expressions of love for God and for others.

- COMMIT your heart and life to the love of God and the love of others, and to praying as an act of loving. *Commit* to praying through the Lord's Prayer twice every day for a week. *Hang* your prayer requests on its various requests.

Recite the Lord's Prayer together

FURTHER EXPLORATION

Ponder the *Shema* and *Kaddish* and how Jesus amended them. *Ponder* how those changes by Jesus change our understanding of prayer. *Journal* your reflections. *Ponder* the following passages of prayers or teachings about prayer:

- Matthew 11:25–27; 26:36–46 • John 17 • Luke 22:31-32; 23:46
- Matthew 27:46 • Luke 11:1–13; 18:1–14

CHAPTER 3

The *Abba* of the *Jesus Creed*

"The difference was that I had for once
really heard with my soul the word that
God loved me just as I was,
with all my anxieties, defeats,
frustrations, and problems."
—Wesley Nelson, *Crying for My Mother*, p. 51.

Recite the *Jesus Creed* together

FORMATION PRINCIPLE:
Abba loves us—this is the premise and
promise of spiritual formation.

FORMATION PRAYER:
*Father, Abba, we are profoundly grateful
that you love us. May we daily bask in that love,
learn that love, and trust that love.
Through Jesus, the Lord. Amen.*

FORMATION EXERCISES:

• IDENTIFY TOGETHER the joys and the difficulties you have in accepting
that *Abba* loves you the way the world's best father loves his children.
Why does our image of God need amending as we learn more about God?

- REFLECT TOGETHER on Jesus' teaching about God as *Abba*. How does it sound in a Jewish world which is more accustomed to addressing God as *Lord* and *reflect together* on what obstacles some of us face in embracing God as *Abba*. *Reflect together* on Wesley Nelson's statement above and his story in *The Jesus Creed*.

- LISTEN deeply to the meaning of the term *Abba* and discover how it can help you understand who God is, what God is like, and how we are to relate to him.

- IMAGINE your relationship to God as *Abba*; imagine how you might behave in God's presence when you comprehend that he is *Abba* for you.

- COMMIT your heart today to accepting God's love for you as an *Abba* love.

Recite the Lord's Prayer together

FURTHER EXPLORATION

Ponder the following prayers of Jesus and how each line reflects God as *Abba*. *Ponder* what each means for one who knows God as *Abba*. *Journal* your reflections.

- Matthew 6:9–13; 11:25-26 • Mark 14:36 • Luke 23:34; 23:46
- John 17 • Mark 15:34–Why is God not addressed here as *Abba*?

The *Jesus Creed* as a Table

"Tables create societies."

Recite the *Jesus Creed* together

F O R M A T I O N   P R I N C I P L E :
At the table of fellowship with Jesus,
where walls between people are broken down,
we find healing, vision, and hope.

F O R M A T I O N   P R A Y E R :
Abba, *awaken in us the power of what your table*
of fellowship has done and is doing for your people.
Awaken in us what your table can do for others—
that it can create healing, grant vision, and enflame
hope. Through Jesus, Lord of the table. Amen.

FORMATION EXERCISES:

- IDENTIFY TOGETHER in your church community the variety and diversity of those who share the table of fellowship. *Identify together* where there are walls between people. *Identify together* those features that make sitting at table together difficult. *Identify together* how Jesus created a vision for a new society at his table. Why are there walls between people? Are some walls good?

- REFLECT TOGETHER on how the table of fellowship can and does embody the vision of Jesus for his people. *Reflect together* on why Jesus was labeled "a glutton and a drunkard" for his table practices. *Reflect together* on whether or not your own practice follows that of Jesus. *Reflect together* on the real differences that make sitting at table difficult. *Reflect together* on the statement: "Tables create societies."

- LISTEN to what the astounding variety of Christians at the same table embodies; the grace it reveals; the challenge it offers.

- IMAGINE a community in which all Christians share a table of fellowship and serve together in the unity that ensues. *Imagine* the role you might play in such a fellowship.

- COMMIT your mind to the message of the table; your heart to the fellowship of the table; your time to the people of the table; and your body to the unity of the table.

Recite the Lord's Prayer together

FURTHER EXPLORATION

Ponder how Jesus' table fellowship practice created problems for both himself and for his followers in the passages below from Luke's Gospel. *Journal* your reflections.

> • Luke 5:27–32; 7:36–50; 9:10–17; 10:8; 12:37; 14:1–14; 15:1-2; 22:7–23 • Notice how table fellowship anticipates the final kingdom (13:29; 14:15–24; 17:8).

CHAPTER 5

A *Creed* of Sacred Love

"Yahweh is the sort who sticks with
what he is stuck with."
—Lewis Smedes, *The Making and
Keeping of Commitments*, p. 9.

Recite the *Jesus Creed* together

FORMATION PRINCIPLE:
Abba *is both loving and holy. His love is sacred.*
Therefore, our love for Abba *is to be sacred.*

FORMATION PRAYER:
Holy Abba, *grant us a vision of your holiness,*
and let it work itself into our whole being,
beginning this day, by inspiring sacredness in our love
for you. Through Jesus, the Lord. Amen.

FORMATION EXERCISES:

- IDENTIFY TOGETHER someone whose love for God is sacred. *Identify together* how your love for God is sacred and how sometimes it is not sacred. *Identify together* how both Hosea and Jesus taught and lived sacred love for God. How do you respond to the graphic imagery in Hosea about God's love for his people?

- REFLECT TOGETHER on the statement by Lewis Smedes. *Reflect together* on your own love for God. Is it sacred or not? *Reflect together* on whether your love for God transforms your speech, provokes repentance, and inspires worship. How can (and do) speech, repentance, and worship express sacred love?

- LISTEN to this biblical expression: "Holy, holy, holy is the LORD ; the whole earth is full of his glory" (Isaiah 6:3). *Listen* also to this: "Holy, holy, holy, the Lord God the Almighty, who was and is and is to come" (Revelation 4:8). *Listen* to how your love for this holy God can be sacred in speech, act, and worship.

- IMAGINE the scene in heaven when the saints sing glory to God for his holiness; *imagine* what life in the Church would be if we were to gain a clearer vision of God's sacred love; *imagine* what your own life would be like if you developed a sacred love for God.

- COMMIT yourself today to contemplating God's sacred love for you more often. *Commit* yourself also to loving *Abba* with a more sacred love.

Recite the Lord's Prayer together

FURTHER EXPLORATION

Ponder how the following people respond to God's sacred love in Luke's Gospel. *Journal* your reflections.

- Peter (Luke 5:1–11); a demonized person (4:31–37); a forgiven woman (7:36–50); Zacchaeus (19:1–10); the disciples at Emmaus (24:13–35)

CHAPTER 6

A *Creed* for Others

"A loving God fosters a loving people."
—Brennan Manning, *The Ragamuffin Gospel,* p. 41.

Recite the *Jesus Creed* together

FORMATION PRINCIPLE:
The Jesus Creed *exhorts us, first, to love God
and, second, to love others.*

FORMATION PRAYER:
Holy Abba, *show us the breadth of your love.
Awaken in us a sensitivity to others. May
your love flow through us to those in our
neighborhoods. Through Jesus Christ, the Lord. Amen.*

FORMATION EXERCISES:

- IDENTIFY TOGETHER how you might be a "Samaritan" in your community and how the Parable of the Good Samaritan deals with the dilemma of a calling and compassion for others. *Identify together* times when an obligation of your calling came into conflict with an opportunity to love another person. *Identify together* a time when you showed "whenever and wherever" love. Why is it difficult to show compassion?

- REFLECT TOGETHER on how you dealt with those situations—how you processed the situation, how you responded, whether or not you think you did what Jesus called you to do, and what you could have done differently. *Reflect together* on Brennan Manning's statement above. *Reflect together* on the difference between "love of *Torah*" and the "*Torah* of love."

- LISTEN to the Lord's prompting as you ponder these situations.

- IMAGINE a similar situation that could occur in the next day or two; in your family, at work, in your community, and in your church life.

- COMMIT yourself now to being a person who strives to love others.

Recite the Lord's Prayer together

FURTHER EXPLORATION

Ponder how Jesus showed "whenever and wherever" love in a variety of situations. *Journal* your reflections.

- Mark 1:40–45 (a leper); 6:30–44; 9:14–32 (healing a boy with an evil spirit) • Matthew 20:29–34 (blind men)
- Luke 7:11–17 (a widow's son)

CHAPTER 7

John the Baptist: The Story of New Beginnings

"The primal word . . . cannot be spoken
too clearly, too wakefully, too explicitly."
—Dietrich von Hildebrand,
Transformation in Christ, p. 69.

Recite the *Jesus Creed* together

FORMATION PRINCIPLE:
*Life begins all over when we tell
God the truth about ourselves.*

FORMATION PRAYER:
Abba, *we come to you just as we are. We fall short
of your call to love you and love others with a
sacred love. Give us the courage to tell you the truth
about ourselves. Through your Spirit's grace reveal to us
our heart so that we might be honest before you.
Through Jesus Christ. Amen.*

FORMATION EXERCISES:

- IDENTIFY TOGETHER how the baptism of John was a "communication event." *Identify together* your struggles about telling the truth to God.

What blocks your willingness to tell the truth about yourself? Do you struggle with spirituality, possessions, or power?

- REFLECT TOGETHER on how John's baptism is like the crossing of the Jordan. *Reflect together* on some situations in your life that are particularly unpleasant, that you have buried into your sub-conscience, and need to open up to God. Remember, God wants you to tell him the truth, and he welcomes truthtellers. *Reflect together* on the statement by von Hildebrand.

- LISTEN to the voice of John who calls us to confess our sins; to the voice of Jesus who invites us to join him in the river; to the voice of the Spirit who searches our hearts; and to the voice of the Father who longs for us to tell the truth.

- COMMIT yourself to truthtelling before God on a regular basis.

- IMAGINE a life where you are honest before God at all times.

Recite the Lord's Prayer together

FURTHER EXPLORATION

Ponder the stories of the following people who learned to tell God the truth in a variety of ways. *Journal* your reflections and responses to truthtelling.

- Peter (Luke 5:1–11) • Matthew, the tax collector (Matthew 9:9–13)
- the sinful woman (Luke 7:36–50) • the Samaritan woman (John 4)
- the woman caught *en flagrant* (John 7:53–8:11)
- Thomas (John 20:24–31)

CHAPTER 8

Joseph:
The Story of
Reputation

"The first thing I was called to give up for God was
what the world calls my fair reputation. . . . and [I]
chose rather to bear contempt with those people of
God, than to enjoy the applause of almost-
Christians for a season."
—George Whitefield, in H. T. Kerr, J. M. Mulder,
Conversions: The Christian Experience
(Grand Rapids: Eerdmans, 1983), p. 62.

Recite the *Jesus Creed* together

FORMATION PRINCIPLE:
*What God thinks of us (our identity) is far more
important than what others think of us (our reputation).*

FORMATION PRAYER:
Abba, *like Joseph your servant, may our identity, rather
than our reputation, shape what we think of ourselves
and how we live. Grant us this day the courage of
Joseph. Through Jesus Christ, your Son. Amen.*

FORMATION EXERCISES

- IDENTIFY TOGETHER how Joseph faced a calling from God that would alter his reputation. *Identify together* a time in your life when reputation and identity were in conflict. Why is our reputation so tenaciously important to us? Reflect on the quotation by George Whitefield.

- REFLECT TOGETHER on how you dealt with that situation—whether good or bad—and what you can learn from that situation. *Reflect together* on how both individuals and groups can worry about reputation and struggle with genuine identity. How can we remind ourselves regularly about the distinction between reputation and identity?

- LISTEN to the voice of God as he speaks to you about identity and reputation.

- IMAGINE how the challenge of reputation and identity might work itself out in the realities of your own immediate future.

- COMMIT your reputation to God so that your identity in following Jesus shapes your life.

Recite the Lord's Prayer together

FURTHER EXPLORATION:

Ponder how the reputation of one or more of the following Gospel characters in Luke was challenged when they identified themselves with Jesus. *Journal* any reflections on your own struggle with identity and reputation.
• Levi (Luke 5:27–32) • the three would-be disciples (9:57–62) • the sinful woman (7:36–50) • Jesus' disciples arguing over greatness (9:46–50) • the Good Samaritan (10:25–37) • the Pharisee and the tax collector (18:9–14)

CHAPTER 9

Mary:
The Story of
Vocation

"Let the Church remember this: that every maker
and worker is called to serve God
in his profession or trade—not outside it."
—Dorothy Sayers, *Creed or Chaos?*, p. 107.

Recite the *Jesus Creed* together

FORMATION PRINCIPLE:
Each of us has a vocation from
God that lets our life speak.

FORMATION PRAYER:
Abba, *take us and our past and turn us into a vocation*
for your glory. Through Jesus Christ, our Lord. Amen.

FORMATION EXERCISES:

- IDENTIFY TOGETHER your struggles with the concept of a vocation in life. *Identify together* what you think God made you (uniquely) to be and to do. *Identify together* someone whom you think has discovered his or her vocation. How can we implement the importance of a vocational understanding of our jobs?

- REFLECT TOGETHER on the sweep of Mary's life: her past, what God called her to do and be, and what impact she has had. *Reflect together* on your past and how God has used it. *Reflect together* on the difference between a "job" and a "vocation." *Reflect together* on the statement from Dorothy Sayers.

- LISTEN to God's promptings for how he can use your life.

- IMAGINE God using you in concrete ways. *Imagine* how God will view your vocation when your life comes to a completion.

- START NOW *to commit your life to Jesus Christ so that you may be constantly "on vocation" for the Lord.*

Recite the Lord's Prayer together

FURTHER EXPLORATION

Ponder the various vocations given by God to various women. *Journal* your reflections on your vocation and how God uses you.

- Elizabeth (Luke 1) • the prophetess Anna (like Mary, an *Anawim* 2:36–38); Mary and Martha (10:38–42) • Martha (John 11)
- Mary (John 12:1–8) • the *Anawim* widow who pleaded for justice (Luke 18:1–8) • the women at the tomb as first witnesses (Luke 24:1–12)

CHAPTER 10

Peter: The Story of Conversion

" . . . the thing I am talking of now may not happen
to everyone in a flash—as it did to St. Paul and
Bunyan: it may be so gradual that
no one could ever point to a particular hour or even
a particular year."
—C. S. Lewis, *Mere Christianity*, p. 128.

Recite the *Jesus Creed* together

FORMATION PRINCIPLE:
*Conversion to Jesus, however suddenly it may begin,
is a life-long process of gentle nods of the soul's
surrender to the* Abba, *a process in which the
person's surrender becomes increasingly public.*

FORMATION PRAYER:
Abba, *we have turned to you, we are turning to you,
and we will turn to you—in our past, in our today,
and in our tomorrow. Through Jesus,
who was utterly surrendered to you. Amen.*

FORMATION EXERCISES:

- IDENTIFY TOGETHER in your own life some "conversion moments," as well as the overall general pattern of conversion. *Identify together* when you think Peter was converted. What are the decisive characteristics (in your group) used to decide when a "conversion" is complete?

- REFLECT TOGETHER on conversion as a series of gentle (or noisy) nods of the soul, for yourself and for others you know. *Reflect together* on the statement above by C. S. Lewis. Discuss how understanding conversion as a process can be misused—both in the call to decision and in the life of following Jesus. *Reflect together* on how your life has been an ongoing transformation.

- LISTEN to the call of Jesus today as he calls you to another day of conversion.

- IMAGINE your day and how some gentle (or noisy) nods of the soul may be needed. *Imagine* your life as continual conversion.

- COMMIT your life today to the conversion this day will need, and to an ongoing conversion.

Recite the Lord's Prayer together

FURTHER EXPLORATION

Ponder once again the life of Peter (as discussed in *The Jesus Creed*) and observe how his life was a life of continual conversion. *Ponder* the following examples of gentle (or noisy) nods of the soul. *Journal* your reflections.

• The first four disciples (Mark 1:16–20) • Matthew, the tax collector (Matthew 9:9–13) • the sinful woman (Luke 7:36–50) • the Samaritan woman (John 4) • the Prodigal Son (Luke 15:11–32) • Zacchaeus (19:1–10) • blind Bartimaeus (Mark 10:46–52)

CHAPTER 11

John:
The Story of
Love

"John was in the Thunderbolt Gang
before he was the Apostle of Love."

Recite the *Jesus Creed* together

FORMATION PRINCIPLE:
The Jesus Creed *calls us to love, but love takes time.*

FORMATION PRAYER:
Abba, *through your love for us and
through your Son's life we learn
what genuine love is. Teach us to love. Give us
time to learn to love. Through Jesus, the Lord. Amen.*

FORMATION EXERCISES:

- IDENTIFY TOGETHER your own story of learning to love. *Identify together* how the apostle John learned to love. *Identify together* some moments when you were more like a thunderbolt. Why is it important to understand Christian growth as a process of growing in love?

- REFLECT TOGETHER on your life as a youth, as a young adult, and in your current phase of life. *Reflect together* on how you have grown in love. *Reflect together* on your life of love. *Reflect together* on the statement about the apostle John. Are there some developmental stages in loving others?

- LISTEN to what the Spirit is saying to you about love, about your life of learning to love, and about your need to grow.

- IMAGINE your life today—at home, at work, with people, and imagine how you can show love to those around you.

- COMMIT to loving others today.

Recite the Lord's Prayer together

FURTHER EXPLORATION

Ponder the following passages from Luke to see how a given person either does or doesn't show love to others. Where might you chart them in a life of learning to love? *Journal* your reflections.

- Mary and Elizabeth (Luke 1:39–45) • Joseph and Mary (2:4–7) • John the Baptist (3:1–18) • people of the Nazareth synagogue (4:14–30) • Levi (or Matthew) (5:27–32) • the Centurion and his friends (7:1–10) • the sinful woman and Simon the Pharisee (7:36–50) • the rich young ruler (18:18–30)

CHAPTER 12

Women:
The Story of
Compassion

"Do ordinary things with extraordinary love:
little things like caring for the sick
and the homeless,
the lonely and the unwanted,
washing and cleaning for them."
—Mother Teresa, in *Mother Teresa: A Simple Path*
(compiled by L. Vardey; New York: Ballantine, 1995),
p. 99.

Recite the *Jesus Creed* together

FORMATION PRINCIPLE:
Compassion is a cycle of God's love
for us and our love for others.

FORMATION PRAYER:
Abba, *in your Son we see compassion alive.*
Quicken our hearts to see with your eyes,
to touch with your hands, and to act with your strength.
Give us eyes to see those around us in need.
Through Jesus, the Lord of compassion. Amen.

FORMATION EXERCISES:

- IDENTIFY TOGETHER how Jesus is compassionate to those in need and what the key features of compassion are. *Identify together* how you have received compassion from others. *Identify together* specific cases when you have been compassionate to others. *Identify together* who is at the margins of your society. Why is compassion both so hard to show and so intensely satisfying when shown to those in need?

- REFLECT TOGETHER on the needs of those who were shown compassion in our chapter. *Reflect together* on what your needs were when you were shown compassion; and on what the needs of others were when you showed compassion. *Reflect together* on Mother Teresa's advice. *Reflect together* on how compassion is inevitable for a follower of Jesus.

- LISTEN to what the Spirit is saying to you about compassion.

- IMAGINE what your society would be like if everyone in need were to be shown compassion.

- COMMIT yourself, as following the *Jesus Creed*, to showing compassion to those in need.

Recite the Lord's Prayer together

FURTHER EXPLORATION

Ponder God's compassionate love and *ponder* the following passages. *Journal* your reflections.

- Elizabeth (Luke 1:7, 13-14, 18, 23–25) and Mary (1:39–45)
- the little ones (Mark 9:42; 10:13–16) • the Beatitudes (Matthew 5:3–12) • a blind man (John 9) • disciples (Mark 6:30–44)

CHAPTER 13

A Society of Transformation

"The kingdom is the society in which
the *Jesus Creed* transforms life."

Recite the *Jesus Creed* together

F O R M A T I O N   P R I N C I P L E :
The kingdom of God is the society where the Jesus Creed
transforms life. That kingdom has arrived in Jesus.

F O R M A T I O N   P R A Y E R :
Abba, *may your kingdom come!*
May your will be done, on earth as it is in heaven!
Stir our hearts to long for your kingdom-will to be
done in this world. Through Jesus, the Lord. Amen.

FORMATION EXERCISES:

- IDENTIFY TOGETHER what Jesus means by "kingdom" by considering
  the Lord's Prayer (Matthew 6:9–13). *Identify together* visible traces of
  the kingdom's transforming powers in your life.

- REFLECT TOGETHER on kingdom now, in your life and in the life of
  others. *Reflect together* on how the kingdom can be seen as "the society

in which the *Jesus Creed* transforms life." Why is the expression "kingdom" so important to Jesus? How do you think "kingdom" relates to Paul's favorite term "church"? Are they the same?

- LISTEN to the word of Jesus: "the kingdom of God is among you" (Luke 17:21); *listen* to what that means for your life; open your life to the kingdom.

- IMAGINE a society totally committed to the *Jesus Creed*; *imagine* what part you will play in that kingdom society; *imagine* your family life in that kingdom; *imagine* your neighborhood and community in that kingdom; *imagine* the world in that kingdom.

- COMMIT yourself today to the central source of that kingdom: fellowship with Jesus, the Person of the kingdom. *Commit* yourself to striving for that kingdom in all that you do.

Recite the Lord's Prayer together

FURTHER EXPLORATION

Ponder the following important texts about the kingdom in the Gospels. *Journal* your reflections about the images "kingdom" evokes for you.

- Matthew 4:17; 11:2–6, 12; 12:28; 16:19 • Mark 4; 10:14-15; 14:25
- Luke 17:20-21

A Society of Mustard Seeds

"Lillian . . . was the real item,
the water of life in a plain tin cup."
—June Sprigg, *Simple Gifts*, p. 90.

Recite the *Jesus Creed* together

F O R M A T I O N   P R I N C I P L E :
*Jesus' model for the kingdom of God is the mustard
seed: a seed that grows among the unlikely, from person
to person, and among the peaceful and patient.*

F O R M A T I O N   P R A Y E R :
Abba, *teach us* your *kingdom ways: that they are not
about power, about glory, or about flash. Show us that
your ways are as subtle and effective as the growth of a
mustard seed. Make us mustard seeds. Through Jesus,
the sower of mustard seeds. Amen.*

FORMATION EXERCISES:

- IDENTIFY TOGETHER your temptations to see the work of God only (or predominantly) in the glorious and powerful. *Identify together* how God's work often moves slowly through the most (seemingly) insignificant ways. Can you identify some examples in your community?

- REFLECT TOGETHER on how the kingdom has grown around you. *Reflect together* on what you would consider to be a true example of the model of the mustard seed. *Reflect together* on the example of Bob Muzikowski as described in *The Jesus Creed*. How is the statement by June Sprigg mustard seed-like?

- LISTEN to what God is saying to you about being a mustard seed in your world. How can you be more mustard seed-like?

- IMAGINE how you might be a mustard seed in some concrete way in your family, in your neighborhood, and in your community. *Imagine* how your church community can become a mustard seed in your community.

- COMMIT your heart and life to what God is saying to you about being a mustard seed; *commit* some of your giving to mustard seed ministries.

Recite the Lord's Prayer together

FURTHER EXPLORATION

Ponder the lives of the following "mustard seeds." *Journal* your reflections.

- Mary (Luke 1) and what she taught Jesus • Joseph (Matthew 1:18–25) and what he taught Jesus
- Peter (Luke 5:1–11 and 1 Peter) • Mary and Martha (Luke 10:38–42 and John 11) • Levi/Matthew (Matthew 9:9–13 and the whole Gospel of Matthew) • the mission of the Twelve (Mark 6:7–13; Matthew 28:16–20; Acts)

A Society for Justice

"Faith works."
—Jim Wallis, *Faith Works*

Recite the *Jesus Creed* together

FORMATION PRINCIPLE:
*The society of the kingdom is a society that
pursues justice because it loves God and others.*

FORMATION PRAYER:
Abba, *grant that we might see that justice is loving God
and loving others and that, in understanding this,
we might pursue justice in our world.
Through Jesus, the establisher of justice. Amen.*

FORMATION EXERCISES:

- IDENTIFY TOGETHER how justice and the *Jesus Creed* are related. *Identify together* an example in your community of someone who lives out the *Jesus Creed* by pursuing justice. How does that person do this? How important is "justice" to Jesus?

- REFLECT TOGETHER on the significance of understanding justice as restitution and as restoration. *Reflect together* on how that difference can reshape your family, your work relationships, your community, and your church. *Reflect together* on the statement by Jim Wallis. How would you define "justice?"

● LISTEN to how you understand what justice means and how others understand it. *Listen* to what God is saying to you about justice.

● IMAGINE what justice would look like in your society if it were defined by the *Jesus Creed.*

● COMMIT yourself to a more biblical understanding of justice. *Commit* yourself to working for justice.

Recite the Lord's Prayer together

FURTHER EXPLORATION

Ponder how justice, as defined by the *Jesus Creed*, is manifest in the following Gospel passages. *Journal* your reflections on the importance of justice to Jesus.

• Luke 4:16–30 • Matthew 5:1–12; 8–9; 25:31–46 • Luke 18:1–8

CHAPTER 16

A Society of Restoration

"Something there is that doesn't love a wall,
That wants it down."
—Robert Frost, "Mending Wall."

Recite the *Jesus Creed* together

FORMATION PRINCIPLE:
The Jesus Creed *empowers us to restore
people to the community.*

FORMATION PRAYER:
Abba, *your kingdom is a kingdom where humans are
restored to fellowship with one another. Forgive us when
we treat others as inferiors. Grant us a renewed vision of
Jesus, the healer, who restores people to his table.
Through Jesus, the Restorer of persons. Amen.*

FORMATION EXERCISES:

- IDENTIFY TOGETHER how the biblical authors think sin and sickness
  can be related. *Identify together* where you find unfair classifications in
  your own mind and practice, as well as in the practice of others. *Identify
  together* where you have broken down walls that separate humans from
  God and from others. How is healing related to community restoration?

- REFLECT TOGETHER on Jesus' practice of healing as he restores people to the kingdom society. *Reflect together* on Robert Frost's famous line about walls (above). Why is it important to look at miracles not only from the angle of their explosive power but also of their lasting impact?

- LISTEN to the voice of Jesus to you and others: "Be healed." *Listen* to the power of Jesus who can restore people.

- IMAGINE a kingdom society in which the "classified" are "de-classified" and welcomed equally to the table of fellowship, where unequal classifications are eliminated. *Imagine* the differences that such a kingdom society would involve.

- COMMIT yourself today to seeing Jesus as the center of the kingdom society and to treating others as restored people.

Recite the Lord's Prayer together

FURTHER EXPLORATION

Ponder the following healing stories about Jesus in the Gospel of Mark. Observe the sorts of ills from which people are released, and give attention especially to what happens to the healed person in society. *Journal* your reflections.

> • Mark 1:29–31; 1:40–45; 2:1–12; 5:1–20; 7:24–30;
> 7:31–37; 8:22–26; 9:14–29; 10:46–52

CHAPTER 17

A Society of Joy

"What distinguishes humanity in creation
is not moral superiority
but the *mark* of a need—
craving to have meaning that is eternal
and thus able to sustain us through
the shifting tides of our years."
—Craig Barnes, *Yearning,* p. 56.

Recite the *Jesus Creed* together

FORMATION PRINCIPLE:
*Humans yearn for the deep joy that comes
from loving God and loving others.*

FORMATION PRAYER:
Abba, *open our minds to see our yearnings.*
Show us what our yearnings are designed to accomplish.
Shape our yearnings so they culminate in loving you
and others, so they become the joy of love.
Through Jesus, the One for whom we yearn. Amen.

FORMATION EXERCISES:

- IDENTIFY TOGETHER some yearnings of people. *Identify together* what Jesus teaches such yearnings are to accomplish. *Identify together* items humans seek as a source of joy. What are some signs of "yearning" in our society?

- REFLECT TOGETHER on the statement by Craig Barnes. *Reflect together* on the meaning of joy as Jesus shows it to us through the wedding wine at Cana. *Reflect on* how C. S. Lewis understood his life as the pursuit of joy. Why is it that such an understanding of joy gives us a deeper understanding of life?

- LISTEN to the yearnings of your heart. *Listen* to them and see how they point toward Jesus Christ.

- IMAGINE those yearnings being shaped toward love of God and love of others, where the deepest joy we find is in abiding in God's love.

- COMMIT your heart to a yearning for the joy that is eternal, for the Joy who is a Person.

Recite the Lord's Prayer together

FURTHER EXPLORATION

Ponder the following passages of the final kingdom and how joy emerges in each case. *Ponder* the "I am" passages in John and notice how joy is a relationship to a Person. *Journal* your reflections.

- Matthew 5:3–12; 8:11; 22:1–14 • Mark 14:25
- John 6:35; 8:12; 10:7; 10:11; 11:25; 14:6; 15:1

A Society with Perspective

"Practice now what you'll have to
put into practice then."
—Thomas à Kempis, *The Imitation of Christ*, p. 49.

"What you think heaven will be is
your perspective on life."

Recite the *Jesus Creed* together

F O R M A T I O N   P R I N C I P L E :
Living the Jesus Creed *means having a perspective on
life in light of the final kingdom, a kingdom noted
especially by fellowship with the* Abba *(love for God)
and with his people (love for others).*

F O R M A T I O N   P R A Y E R :
Abba, *grant us a vision of eternal life so that we may
live now in light of that eternity. Awaken in us a love
for you and for your people. Give us this perspective.
Through Jesus, the Lord of fellowship. Amen.*

FORMATION EXERCISES:

- IDENTIFY TOGETHER how you conceive of heaven (or the final kingdom). *Identify together* what Jesus says the final kingdom will be like.

- REFLECT TOGETHER on how your conception of heaven shapes your life today. *Reflect together* on how Jesus' view of eternity can re-shape your life to give you perspective. *Reflect together* on the quotations. How does one's view of the final kingdom shape one's life now?

- LISTEN to the theme that fellowship with God and others is for all eternity. *Listen to* what God is saying to you today about the importance of that fellowship.

- IMAGINE perfect fellowship with the *Abba* and his people; *imagine* that fellowship shaping your family, your friends, and your church community.

- COMMIT yourself to a life devoted to fellowship with the *Abba* and his people.

Recite the Lord's Prayer together

FURTHER EXPLORATION

Ponder the following final kingdom scenes of the Bible. *Journal* your reflections.

- Mark 14:25 • Matthew 25:31–46 • 1 Corinthians 15
- 1 Thessalonians 4–5 • Revelation 4–5; 20–22
- compare to Genesis 1–2

CHAPTER 19

Believing in Jesus

"And, no matter how much we love *theology*—
it will never love us back."
—Mark Allan Powell, *Loving Jesus,* p. 53.

"The goal of a disciple is not perfection
but relationship."

Recite the *Jesus Creed* together

FORMATION PRINCIPLE:
*To believe in Jesus means to live in personal
relationship with him—in mind, body, and heart.*

FORMATION PRAYER:
Abba, *purge us of identifying you with abstractions
and theological formulas. Replace our abstractions
with your personal presence. Through Jesus,
your incarnate Son. Amen.*

FORMATION EXERCISES:

- IDENTIFY TOGETHER what it means to "believe." *Identify together* what Jesus means by "believe." *Identify together* how the "friends of faith" are dimensions of genuine faith.

- REFLECT TOGETHER on temptations in your life to reduce "believing" to Christian orthodox thinking, to activism, or to persistence. *Reflect together* on how you need to let "believing" be first of all a personal relationship to God through Jesus. *Reflect together* on the two quotations above. *Reflect on* how Benjamin Franklin understood the "moral life."

- LISTEN to the personal significance of Jesus' word: "Come, follow *me*" (Mark 1:17). *Hear* what God is saying to you about relating to him—in heart, mind, and body.

- IMAGINE your life working itself out from a center that begins with a relationship with God.

- COMMIT your life once again to a gentle and vulnerable relationship with God.

Recite the Lord's Prayer together

FURTHER EXPLORATION

Ponder the following examples of how Jesus makes our relationship to him central (and how that relationship is a relationship to God). *Journal* your reflections.

- Matthew 10:26–33, 40–42; 25:31–46 • Mark 10:35–45
- Luke 10:38–42 • John 1:12; 3:16; 4; 6; 15

Abiding in Jesus

"I do this simply by keeping my attention
on God and by being generally
and lovingly aware of Him."
—Brother Lawrence,
The Practice of the Presence of God, p. 93.

Recite the *Jesus Creed* together

F O R M A T I O N   P R I N C I P L E :
*The "one thing needful" for spiritual formation
is constantly attending to Jesus—
heart, soul, mind, and strength.*

F O R M A T I O N   P R A Y E R :
Abba, *may our heart, mind, soul, and strength be
constantly available to the flow of your presence.
Now and forevermore. Through Jesus, the Lord. Amen.*

FORMATION EXERCISES:

- IDENTIFY TOGETHER what percentage of the day you think you are "attending to" or "abiding in" Jesus. Be honest. *Identify together* what distracts you, what breaks down your attending to Jesus and abiding in Jesus. *Identify together* your habits for reading the Bible, for worship, and for fellowship with other Christians. *Identify together* if your reading is "informational" or "formational." Why is regular Bible reading so important to living out the *Jesus Creed*?

- REFLECT TOGETHER on Brother Lawrence's statement (above). *Reflect together* on what Jesus says about the "one needful thing" and on what "abiding" means. *Reflect together* on your own practice of abiding. *Reflect together* on reading the Bible more "formationally."

- LISTEN to the words of Jesus: "Remain in me and I will remain in you" (John 15:4a). Do you genuinely believe these words? Do you hear these words as a promise from Jesus to you?

- IMAGINE what your day will be like when you "attend to" Jesus and "abide in" Jesus constantly. *Imagine* what you will do when you forget about God's presence, and how you will open up your heart to abiding again. *Imagine* improvement in formational and informational Bible reading, in worship, and in fellowship.

- COMMIT this day, this morning, this next hour, these next few minutes to abiding constantly in Jesus. It doesn't happen accidentally. *Commit* yourself to reading the Word of God daily, worshiping God regularly, and participating in fellowship with those who love God and others.

Recite the Lord's Prayer together

FURTHER EXPLORATION

Ponder the following verses, one at a time, in a formational mode of reading. *Journal* your reflections.

- John 15:1, 4, 5, 6, 7, 9

CHAPTER 21

Surrendering in Jesus

"Only if we serve, will we experience freedom.
Only if we lose ourselves in loving,
will we find ourselves.
Only if we die to our own self-centredness,
will we begin to live."
—John R. W. Stott, *The Incomparable Christ,* p. 89.

Recite the *Jesus Creed* together

FORMATION PRINCIPLE:
*We love God (by following Jesus) and we love
others only when we surrender to God and to
others personally, mentally, and physically.*

FORMATION PRAYER:
Abba, *remind us that our fear of surrender prevents
us from loving you and others as we ought.
Awaken us to live for loving you and others.
Through Jesus, the Lord. Amen.*

FORMATION EXERCISES:

- IDENTIFY TOGETHER how surrender and love are connected. *Identify together* where you are in the "surrender" dimension of loving God and others. *Identify together* what is holding you back. *Identify together* how you can surrender to God personally, mentally, and physically. Why is the word "surrender" unpopular today?

- REFLECT TOGETHER on your deepest loves—your family members, your spouse, and your best friends. Observe how some forms of surrender are part of all genuine love. *Reflect together* on the wise words of John Stott in the quotation. *Reflect together* on how you might surrender your mind more to the Bible, to Church history, and to spiritual formation.

- LISTEN to the Spirit's promptings that you may surrender more completely and therefore love more completely. *Listen* to the boundaries of surrender for you personally.

- IMAGINE your life as a life of surrender to God and to others, and *imagine* how such surrender can flood your life with joy.

- COMMIT yourself today to concrete acts of surrender to God and to others.

Recite the Lord's Prayer together

FURTHER EXPLORATION

Ponder how the following people surrendered themselves to the *Jesus Creed* of loving God and others. *Journal* your reflections.

- Zechariah (Luke 1:5–25) • Mary (Luke 1:26–38) • Peter (Luke 5:1–11)
  - Matthew (Matthew 9:9–13) • Mary and Martha (Luke 10:38–42)
    - a healed man (John 5:1–15) • Nicodemus (John 3:1–15; 19:38–42)
      - Mary Magdalene (Luke 8:1–3; Mark 15:42–16:8)

CHAPTER 22

Restoring in Jesus

"We worked at it, prayed about it,
deliberately set about serving one another
and allowed others to help us—
and, because of these things,
the marriage was restored and is
the joy of our lives today."
—Michael Green, *Adventure of Faith*, p. 69.

Recite the *Jesus Creed* together

FORMATION PRINCIPLE:
Failure to live out the Jesus Creed *is real;*
restoration can also be real.

FORMATION PRAYER:
Abba, *we have failed in our love for you and for others.*
Forgive us. Restore us. Through Jesus, the Lord. Amen.

FORMATION EXERCISES:

- IDENTIFY TOGETHER one or two (or more if you'd like) times when you've failed to love God or others. *Identify together* your response and the aftermath. *Identify together* one major social "disease" to which you are sensitive and assess your own part in that problem. Why is failure, or sin, not talked about today?

- REFLECT TOGETHER on the reality of failure and the goodness of God's forgiveness in the life of Jesus' disciples. *Reflect* together on the example of Michael Green's marriage problems in *The Jesus Creed*. What can you learn from Michael and his wife? Reflect *together* on your own experiences of failure and restoration. *Reflect together* on the "pattern of imperfection."

- LISTEN to the Spirit's sifting of your heart, and how you might rectify those situations. *Listen* for promptings of both repentance and restitution.

- IMAGINE a world where humans are genuinely restored to one another.

- COMMIT yourself to a life of truthtelling about failure and about being restored.

Recite the Lord's Prayer together

FURTHER EXPLORATION

Ponder one or more of the following passages involving restoration. *Journal* your reflections from Mark's Gospel.

- Mark 4:10, 13, 33–34; 7:17; 8:16–21: failure to understand Jesus' teachings • 4:35–41: screaming out in fear during a storm • 6:35–37; 8:4: blindness about Jesus' ability to provide provisions • 7:24–30; 10:13–16: inability to accept Gentiles and children • 9:14–19: inability to trust God to heal
- 10:32: fear of not having God's protection • 10:35–45: yearning for most valuable status among apostles • 14:37, 40, 54, 66–72: afraid to support Jesus in his passion

CHAPTER 23

Forgiving in Jesus

"Every one says forgiveness is a lovely idea,
until they have something to forgive."
—C. S. Lewis, *Mere Christianity*, p. 104.

Recite the *Jesus Creed* together

FORMATION PRINCIPLE:
Those who live the Jesus Creed *forgive others.*

FORMATION PRAYER:
Abba, *we have sinned before you—in heart, in soul, in mind, and in strength. Yet, in your grace you forgive us. Grant us the grace to forgive others with the forgiveness we have received from you, as Jesus himself has done. Through Jesus, the Lord. Amen.*

FORMATION EXERCISES:

- IDENTIFY TOGETHER how forgiveness moves from God to you and from you to others. *Identify together* your own sinfulness and your own forgiveness by God. *Identify together* times when you've forgiven others and when others have forgiven you. *Identify together* those in your life you need to think of forgiving. *Identify together* the value of distinguishing "objective" and "subjective" forgiveness. *Identify together* the value of distinguishing a "system of justice" and a "system of forgiveness." What is forgiveness? Why is forgiveness easier to talk about than to practice?

- REFLECT TOGETHER on God's pre-emptive strike of grace and forgiveness. *Reflect together* on the *Jesus Creed* as a disposition of love toward all, even those who have done you wrong. *Reflect together* on those who have hurt you—whether in heart, soul, mind, or strength—and ponder how you should respond. *Reflect together* on C. S. Lewis's statement above. *Reflect together* on the need to tell the truth and protect your own integrity in forgiving someone. *Reflect together* on the story of Simon Wiesenthal from *The Jesus Creed.* What would you have done? Why do we need to be patient with those who need to forgive?

- LISTEN to what the Lord would have you do.

- IMAGINE your way into your own hurts and into a situation where you can forgive those whom you need to forgive.

- COMMIT your heart and life to a disposition of forgiveness; ask God for grace and strength.

Recite the Lord's Prayer together

FURTHER EXPLORATION

Ponder the following passage one more time. *Journal* your reflections.

- John 21

CHAPTER 24

Reaching Out
in Jesus

"God's church exists not for itself
but for the benefit of those who
are not yet members. . . .
[and] the church which lives for itself
will be sure to die by itself."
—Michael Green, *Adventure of Faith*, pp. 29, 88.

Recite the *Jesus Creed* together

FORMATION PRINCIPLE:
Living the Jesus Creed *means reaching out
with the mission of Jesus to others.*

FORMATION PRAYER:
Abba, *make us a physical and verbal witness
of your Son. Through Jesus, the Lord. Amen.*

FORMATION EXERCISES:

- IDENTIFY TOGETHER how the mission of Jesus is the mission of a disciple. *Identify together* on a scale from one to ten how you would rate yourself as one who either does (one) or does not (ten) reach out with the mission of Jesus to others. *Identify together* your primary mode (physically, verbally) of reaching out to others. Discuss what "reaching out" means.

- REFLECT TOGETHER on what mode of reaching out you see in Peter and Mary Magdalene. *Reflect together* on what guides you in your mode of reaching out. Why is it hard to reach out?

- LISTEN to the Spirit's guidance when it comes to reaching out with the mission of Jesus. In all the early Christian evidence, the Spirit prompted early Christians to declare Jesus Christ to others with a Spirit-inspired boldness. Ask God's Spirit to embolden your witness.

- IMAGINE one situation today and how you will reach out with the mission of Jesus. What will you do? What will you say? Are you ready?

- COMMIT your life to being one that reaches out to others with the mission of Jesus.

Recite the Lord's Prayer together

FURTHER EXPLORATION

Ponder the missionary chapter *par excellence* in the Gospels: Matthew 10. How does each passage speak to a different dimension of reaching out to others? Think through the following passages. *Journal* your reflections.

• Matthew 9:36–38: the need • Matthew 10:1: the enablement
• 10:5-6: the location • 10:7: the message • 10:8: the actions • 10:9-10: the provision • 10:11–16: the reputation • 10:17–25: the opposition
• 10:26–39: the mental readiness • 10:40–42: the promise

In the Jordan with Jesus

"But if he, Jesus, is to do all this [rescue his people],
this is how he must do it:
by humbly identifying himself with God's people,
by taking their place, sharing their penitence, living
their life and ultimately dying their death."
—Tom Wright, *Matthew for Everyone,* 1.21-22.

Recite the *Jesus Creed* together

F O R M A T I O N   P R I N C I P L E :
*In the Jordan, Jesus repented for us and we
are called to join Jesus in his repentance.*

F O R M A T I O N   P R A Y E R :
Abba, *our own confession is inadequate and shallow.
We are, however, grateful Jesus has confessed for us.
We turn our confession over to him.
Through Jesus, the Lord of the true confession. Amen.*

FORMATION EXERCISES

- IDENTIFY TOGETHER some ways you have understood Jesus' baptism in the Jordan. *Identify together* how understanding it as a perfect repentance can be helpful. Why is it important that Jesus repent for us?

- REFLECT TOGETHER on the story in *The Jesus Creed* about a father shoveling through snow for a child. *Reflect together* on the significance of the term "repentance" in explaining what John's baptism meant, and how Jesus entered the Jordan in such a baptism for you. *Reflect together* on Tom Wright's statement above. *Reflect together* on your own repentance: its adequacies and inadequacies.

- LISTEN to the Father's word: "This is my beloved Son," and hear how that approving word sets the tone for Jesus' repentance for us.

- IMAGINE your repentance as part of his perfect repentance.

- COMMIT yourself to a renewed understanding of how repentance works, and how you can see your repentance as continual participation in Jesus' repentance for you.

Recite the Lord's Prayer together

FURTHER EXPLORATION

Ponder how your baptism is a participation in Jesus' baptism, and how your repentance is perfected by Jesus' baptism. *Journal* your reflections.

- Compare Matthew 3:13–17 and Romans 6:1–14.
- Read John 1:29–34 and observe what the baptism of Jesus reveals.

CHAPTER 26

In the Wilderness with Jesus

"Jesus is tempted in the wilderness for a reason:
he must relive Israel's wilderness test,
pass those tests, so he can enter
into the Land as the Obedient Israelite—
and do so for us."

Recite the *Jesus Creed* together

FORMATION PRINCIPLE:

*Jesus was tempted and obeyed for us, so we can join him
in his perfect obedience—in his perfect trust, his perfect
patience, and in his perfect worship. His obedience is
ours because his obedience is imputed to us.*

FORMATION PRAYER:

*Abba, we confess that we rely upon our own resources to
overcome temptation far too often. Instead, bring into
our mind the perfect obedience of Jesus so that we might
take courage in his obedience for us. Through Jesus
Christ, the Lord. Amen.*

FORMATION EXERCISES:

- IDENTIFY TOGETHER some ways you have understood Jesus' temptation in the wilderness. *Identify together* how understanding it as "active" obedience on your behalf helps you. *Identify together* how the temptation of Jesus is an act of love for both God and for you. *Identify together* some examples of someone being tested prior to the completion of the goal. Why is it important that Jesus be tested for you?

- REFLECT TOGETHER on the significance of the term "obedience" (in trust, in patience, and in worship) as explaining what the temptation of Jesus was about. *Reflect together* on your own trust, patience, and worship—on their adequacies and inadequacies. *Reflect together* on how the "active" obedience of Christ for you does not relieve you of the responsibility to obey.

- LISTEN to what the Bible says: "Jesus was led by the Spirit into the desert" (Matthew 4:1). Hear how that sets the tone for what the temptation of Jesus was all about. *Listen* to how the temptation of Jesus is a "second wilderness" experience and how a test sometimes precedes the reward.

- IMAGINE your obedience as part of Jesus' perfect obedience. In particular, imagine your trust, your patience, and your worship as swallowed up in Jesus' perfect trust, patience, and worship.

- COMMIT yourself to perceiving your obedience as part of Jesus' perfect obedience.

Recite the Lord's Prayer together

FURTHER EXPLORATION

Ponder how your temptations were undertaken by Jesus, and how his response to temptations needs to set the tone for your response. *Ponder* the response of Peter to temptation in Mark 14. *Journal* your reflections.

CHAPTER 27

On the Mountain with Jesus

"Next to the Blessed Sacrament itself,
your neighbour is the holiest object
presented to your senses."
—C. S. Lewis, *The Weight of Glory*, p. 15.

Recite the *Jesus Creed* together

FORMATION PRINCIPLE:
*Jesus revealed the glory of our true humanity
and the glory of his own Sonship to encourage
us to endure suffering and death.*

FORMATION PRAYER:
Abba, *we want neither suffering nor death. But,
because of your Son's revelation of the glory that is in us
and the glory that awaits us, we can face each day,
knowing that the glory exceeds the suffering and the
death. Grant us the grace of seeing through other people
to the glory you have planted in them. Through Jesus,
the Lord. Amen.*

FORMATION EXERCISES:

- IDENTIFY TOGETHER how you understand the Transfiguration. *Identify together* what role, if any, the Transfiguration plays in Christian thinking. Why is the Transfiguration important?

- REFLECT TOGETHER on how the Transfiguration as an event *for us* can re-shape our understanding of both the Transfiguration and how we face suffering and death. *Reflect together* on the statement by C. S. Lewis. *Reflect together* on some people you know who have a "Transfiguration perspective" on suffering and death.

- LISTEN to your heart and how it responds to the fear of suffering and death. How does the Father's word, "This is My Son whom I have chosen," embolden you as you face suffering and death? *Listen* to what the Lord says to you.

- IMAGINE facing suffering or death. Put yourself in the homes of those you know who have recently experienced suffering and death, and *imagine* how you might respond redemptively in light of what the Transfiguration is all about.

- COMMIT your heart and your emotions to responding to the threats of suffering and death with the good news of Jesus' Transfiguration for us.

Recite the Lord's Prayer together

FURTHER EXPLORATION

Ponder how the Transfiguration relates to other major events in the life of Jesus. *Journal* your reflections.

- Compare the Transfiguration of Jesus and the Cross scene: Matthew 17:1–8 and 27:32–56. Notice similarities and differences, comparisons and contrasts.
  - Read John 11 and observe how Jesus faces death. Relate this to the Transfiguration.
- Read 1 Corinthians 15 and compare the resurrection of the "body" in Paul's letter to Jesus' body in the Transfiguration.
  - Discuss the significance of Moses and Elijah appearing at the Transfiguration scene: read Deuteronomy 18; Exodus 34; and 1 Kings 18–19; Malachi 3–4.

At the Last Supper
with Jesus

"Taste and see."
—Tim Dearborn, *Taste and See*

Jesus didn't give us a theory of the atonement
but "an act to perform . . . a meal that speaks
more volumes than any theory."
—Tom Wright, *Luke for Everyone,* p. 262.

Recite the *Jesus Creed* together

F O R M A T I O N P R I N C I P L E :
*Jesus has offered us a token of his body and his
blood, in the elements of the Lord's Supper, so we can
establish a rhythm of remembrance.*

F O R M A T I O N P R A Y E R :
Holy Abba, *we stand before you, with these much-needed
elements in our hands and before our eyes, and we thank
you for this rhythm of remembrance. It evokes in our
memories what you have done for us through the gift of
your Son. Through Jesus, the Lord. Amen.*

FORMATION EXERCISES:

- IDENTIFY TOGETHER how you understand the Last Supper of Jesus; how you understand the practice of Communion, the Eucharist, or Mass; and what you can learn by connecting this to Israel's practice of annually observing Passover. *Identify together* how you understand the value of ritual, routine, and rhythm. *Identify together* how the Last Supper is an act (by Jesus) of love for God and for others. *Identify together* how it is also our act of love for God and for others.

- REFLECT TOGETHER on the meaning of the term "remember." *Reflect together* on the meaning of "this is my body" and "this cup is the new covenant in my blood." *Reflect together* on the statements by Tim Dearborn and Tom Wright, and how they apply to the Lord's Supper.

- LISTEN to what the Lord is saying to you about the need to establish the rhythm of remembering Jesus Christ.

- IMAGINE your way back to the Last Supper of Jesus; think of the room, the U-shaped arrangement of the tables, how you are reclining next to Jesus; think of the lighting; think of the evening and what Passover night signifies. *Imagine* hearing Jesus' words of institution.

- COMMIT yourself to a rhythm of remembrance of Jesus, as he gave himself to you in the Last Supper, as a revolutionary reinterpretation of Passover.

Recite the Lord's Prayer together

FURTHER EXPLORATION

Ponder how our celebration of the Lord's Supper is an ingestion of all that Jesus has done for us, because it reinterprets the Passover meal celebration. *Journal* your reflections.

- Examine 1 Corinthians 5:7 and explain what Paul means when he says, "Get rid of the old yeast that you may be a new batch without yeast—as you really are. For Christ, our Passover lamb, has been sacrificed."
- Read Exodus 12. What are the various elements of the Passover meal? Try to understand each one, and why each is done.
- Read Luke 22:7–23 and jot down each similarity and dissimilarity to Passover.
- Read 1 Corinthians 10–11 and *ponder* how the Lord's Supper expresses the gospel, the central importance of the death of Jesus, and the unity of the Church.

CHAPTER 29

At the Cross
with Jesus

"There are ages," she says, "when it is
possible too woo the reader;
there are others when something
more drastic is necessary."
—Flannery O'Connor, *Complete Works*, p. 820.

"There is no Christianity without the cross, the
cross that carries us and the cross that we carry."
—Gordon Wakefield, *Bunyan the Christian*, p. 79.

Recite the *Jesus Creed* together

FORMATION PRINCIPLE:
*The cross Jesus endured reveals God's love for
us as physical sympathy, spiritual protection,
and moral transformation.*

FORMATION PRAYER:
Abba, *grant that we may see the magnitude of the Cross.
That we may see your love for us. That we may see that
you know our pain, that you have rescued us from sin,
and that you offer us a new path for life. That we may
see that it took a grotesque cross for you to exhibit this,
your love for us. Through Jesus, the Lord. Amen.*

FORMATION EXERCISES:

- IDENTIFY TOGETHER how repulsive the Cross is to you. *Identify together* how you have at times cheapened the Cross. *Identify together* how comprehensive your view of the Cross is.

- REFLECT TOGETHER on the physical pain endured by Jesus. *Reflect together* on the moment when the sun turned dark and the temple veil was split and Jesus cries out "My God, my God, why you have abandoned me?" *Reflect together* on the statements by Flannery O'Connor and Gordon Wakefield. How do their views of the Cross help us understand the Cross? *Reflect together* on the various ways Christians have kept the Cross before them: wearing a cross, using the sign of the cross, etc.

- LISTEN to what the Spirit is saying to you about the magnitude of the Cross for Christian faith.

- IMAGINE this day as a day shaped by the Cross: your work, your travel, your conversations, your eating, your family life, and your evening.

- COMMIT your heart, soul, mind, and strength to a greater appreciation of the Cross.

Recite the Lord's Prayer together

FURTHER EXPLORATION

Ponder the following passages about the Cross, thinking through each one methodically in light of the Cross as physical sympathy, spiritual rescue, and moral transformation. Begin by reading these verses: Luke 9:23; Romans 3:21–26. *Journal* your reflections.

• Galatians 2:15–21 and 3:10–14 • Romans 5:12–21 • 1 Peter 2:21–25
• Hebrews 5:1–10; 7:11–28 • Revelation 5:1–14

CHAPTER 30

At the Tomb
with Jesus

"God did not abolish the fact of evil:
He transformed it.
He did not stop the Crucifixion:
He rose from the dead."
—Dorothy Sayers, *Creed or Chaos?*, p. 24.

Recite the *Jesus Creed* together

FORMATION PRINCIPLE:
*The resurrection of Jesus transforms
our disasters into new life.*

FORMATION PRAYER:
Abba, *on this day we express our deepest praise for
the power of the resurrection, for raising Jesus Christ
from among the dead as the firstborn among all those
who will follow him in the resurrection.
Through Jesus Christ, Lord of the living. Amen.*

FORMATION EXERCISES:

- IDENTIFY TOGETHER the various arguments for the resurrection and which ones are most compelling to you. *Identify together* how you have responded to disasters in your life. *Identify together* if your responses were like the disciples' little disasters or if they were similar to how they embraced the resurrection. How is the resurrection important in the day-to-day struggles of life—in the big issues of life?

- REFLECT TOGETHER on how the resurrection of Jesus is an expression of God's love for us. *Reflect together* on how you have learned the resurrection perspective on life's disasters. *Reflect together* on the statement by Dorothy Sayers. *Reflect together* on the story of Margaret Kim Peterson.

- LISTEN to what God is saying to you about your disasters; to what he is saying to you *through* your disasters.

- IMAGINE your day as a day of living in the resurrection of Christ: How will you begin your day? How will you conduct yourself with others? How will you approach your vocation? How will you relate to your family?

- COMMIT your heart, soul, mind, and strength to a resurrection perspective.

Recite the Lord's Prayer together

FURTHER EXPLORATION

Ponder the power of the resurrection by comparing Mark 15; John 20-21; Acts 1 with Acts 2–5. Notice the change in attitude, belief, and behavior on the part of those who are mentioned. *Journal* your reflections.